William the Conqueror
and the Battle of Hastings

Michael St John Parker

D1399069

1066 *is surely the best-known date in English history;*
for some people, in fact, it may be the only date they know.
And the popular instinct is sound, for the importance of the year
matches its fame – 1066 saw a decisive step in the evolution
of the English nation.

Previously, England had been no more than a geographical expression,
a territory divided into warring principalities.
After 1066, the nation-state was an emerging reality.
This was the largely accidental achievement of
William the Conqueror.

William's Norman Origins

below
Falaise Castle, the Conqueror's birthplace, showing the 12th-century keep and, in front, the 13th-century cylindrical great-tower of Philip II.

For some three and a half centuries, Viking sea-raiders from Scandinavia terrorized the people of western Europe. At first they came as plunderers, then as settlers and traders, but always they were fierce and dangerous. Their light dragon ships were equally at home in the North Sea and in the river estuaries which led them inland to seize strongpoints, from which they fanned out over the countryside.

Early in the 10th century, one of these war-bands, led by a certain Rollo, captured the town of Rouen on the River Seine, and secured a grant of territory from the then king of the Franks. Rollo and his descendants were as cunning as they were formidable,

imposing their power equally on Frankish natives and fresh waves of Vikings, so that by the early 11th century they ruled a vast tract which had come to be called *terra Normannorum*, the land of the men from the north.

Rollo's great-grandson, Richard II (996–1026), was the first regularly to call himself 'Duke of the Normans'. By then the little state was prosperous and strong, enjoying a rich agriculture and a vigorous commercial life focused on the capital, Rouen. The Normans were proud of their distinctive origins, but they had become more French than Scandinavian in their manners, customs and language; in particular, they had been converted to the Christian faith, though they sometimes found

it convenient to ignore the details of its etiquette.

English connections were almost as important as French in the life of the duchy, and Duke Richard's sister, Emma, was married to the Saxon king, Aethelred the Unready. As a result, when Aethelred and his family were forced to flee from marauding Danes in 1013, they took refuge in Normandy, where Aethelred's son, later to be King Edward the Confessor, stayed when his parents returned to face a hazardous future in England.

Richard II was succeeded as duke first by his elder son, Richard III (1026–27) and then by the younger, Robert. Robert's reign was unsettled; there were troubles on his frontiers,

and disturbances among his subjects – notwithstanding which, he imprudently set out on a pilgrimage to Jerusalem early in 1035, in the course of which he died, still unmarried. His designated heir was his illegitimate son William, who had been born at Falaise in late 1027 or early 1028, the result of a liaison with a certain Herleva, daughter of a tanner – or, as some accounts have it, an undertaker.

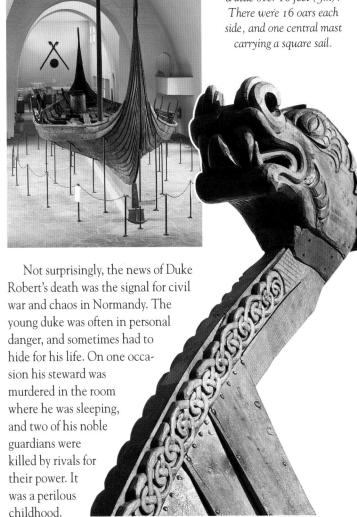

below
The figurehead of a Viking longship, from Oslo. Such dragon-heads were often brightly painted or gilded. The ships themselves were sometimes called 'dragon ships'.

left
The Viking ship discovered at Gokstad, near Oslo, in 1880. About 80 feet (25m) long, it broadens amidships to a little over 16 feet (5m). There were 16 oars each side, and one central mast carrying a square sail.

Not surprisingly, the news of Duke Robert's death was the signal for civil war and chaos in Normandy. The young duke was often in personal danger, and sometimes had to hide for his life. On one occasion his steward was murdered in the room where he was sleeping, and two of his noble guardians were killed by rivals for their power. It was a perilous childhood.

Saxon England: A Disputed Succession

below

Harold Godwineson seen swearing an oath, on sacred relics and in the presence of witnesses, to assist Duke William, who is seen sitting on his throne and carrying a sceptre. A scene from the Bayeux Tapestry, which gives a decidedly Norman view of the events surrounding the conquest – although ironically it has been established that the work of embroidery was almost certainly carried out by English hands. The tapestry was commissioned by Odo, Bishop of Bayeux, Duke William's half-brother and one of his chief supporters.

The kingdom of England in the middle of the 11th century was rich, civilized and vulnerable. It had been created by the interaction of Viking invasions and Saxon resistance; the Vikings destroyed all but one of the Saxon tribal monarchies, but the surviving house of Wessex then triumphed over all. Its population of some two million, dwelling in rich farmlands and prosperous trading towns, benefited from the circulation of a national silver coinage which was as reliable in value as it was distinguished in design. Its kings made general laws as well as dispensing justice in individual cases, using the services of a developed secretariat. Shires and their subdivisions, known as hundreds, provided local government strongly based on customary law and popular consent. There were procedures for raising armies, fleets and national taxes. The Church was rich, well-organized and often learned. In the decorative arts particularly, English skill and wealth combined, to the envy of western Europe.

Envy was easily translated into grasping action. Viking marauders returned in strength from the late 10th century onwards, and in 1016 King Cnut (Canute) of Denmark succeeded where all his predecessors had failed, by killing Aethelred of Wessex and seizing the crown of all England. This Scandinavian ascendancy was abruptly ended by the early death and childlessness of Cnut's son Harthacnut (1035–42), but other predators lurked close by.

To succeed Harthacnut, the English magnates brought back from exile the prince who had formerly taken refuge at the Norman court, Edward, the son of Aethelred. Edward the Confessor, as he became known for his patronage of the Church, found his unexpected kingship uncomfortable. Brought up in exile, he was an idler and an opportunist; Saxon he may have been by birth, but he seemed to his new subjects very French, or more specifically Norman. And it was doubtless the Norman influence which prevailed when, around 1051, he made some form of promise to William of Normandy that he should have the reversion of the English throne. Such a promise was not as extraordinary or irregular then as it might seem now. Saxon kingship was not decided simply on hereditary right, important though

VBI hAROLD:SACRAMENTVM:FECIT: hIC hAROLD:DVX VVILLELMO DVCI:-

that was, of course: the support of powerful families, and the known wishes of a predecessor, were also important factors. Edward the Confessor had no child, but plenty of potential heirs, and the need to balance the forces competing for power at his court made him willing to offer his blessing to various candidates from time to time. In 1051 he was engaged in a complex struggle with the family of his overmighty subject Godwine, Earl of Wessex – hence the 'promise' to William, who offered the prospect of a counterpoise. Later on, the sons of

to the English throne. Harold later repudiated the oath, as having been extracted under duress; but William insisted on its validity, and made it a charge against Harold that his acceptance of the crown had involved an act of perjury.

It is not possible to be certain of the rights and wrongs of this oath at a distance of 900 years, but it seems unlikely that William saw it as much more than a useful prop for his ambitions, or that it troubled Harold's Saxon subjects.

above
A silver penny minted at Chester during the reign of King Edward the Confessor. The Saxon coinage was exceptionally fine.

left
Anglo-Saxon harvest scene. The agricultural wealth of England made it attractive to Duke William's land-hungry adventurers.

below
King Edward the Confessor feasts in royal state. Pages bring dishes to his table, while courtiers attend him – or collapse exhausted at his feet!

Godwine achieved too much power to be gainsaid, and Edward bestowed his deathbed blessing on the most formidable of them, Harold. But the earlier 'promise' had not been forgotten – indeed, William found it far too convenient to his own ambitions to lay it aside lightly.

A further and perhaps specially embittering factor was introduced into the situation in 1064/5, when Harold Godwineson, journeying to France, fell into William's hands and was persuaded – or tricked – into swearing an oath of fealty to William, and promising to assist William's succession

above
A coin minted during Harold's brief reign and bearing his effigy.

below
Harold enthroned with orb and sceptre, while a courtier bears aloft the sword of state. Archbishop Stigand stands beside the throne.

harold Godwineson was crowned king of England in Westminster Abbey on 6 January, 1066. He had exerted his family's great wealth and power, and his own forcefulness, in a swift, decisive, opportunist fashion which seems to have been characteristic.

William of Normandy was playing an altogether longer game, one that went back 15 years or more. The threatened child who had had to lurk and run for his life in Normandy's civil wars had matured into one of the toughest soldiers and astutest politicians in France. A series of battles and sieges, from Val-ès-Dunes in 1047 onwards, had earned him a reputation as a formidable warrior, a skilled tactician and a dynamic leader. His cunning in diplomacy was similarly attested by a trail of broken hostile coalitions and a growing array of allies and vassals. He had put Normandy thoroughly into order, so that it was well-governed, wealthy and powerful; but his ambitions went much further than that.

William's lust for conquest was not unusual in itself; on the contrary, it was characteristic of the French nobility who rampaged through Spain, Italy and the Middle East in the 11th and 12th centuries. What was distinctive about William of Normandy was his efficiency in matching means to ends, and turning dreams into realities.

So William assembled his supporters at various centres throughout Normandy in the earlier part of 1066 and expounded his plans. He covered his back towards France. He canvassed the Pope, who sent a banner to display his support. He built ships, gathered weapons, collected munitions and supplies. 'His leading councillors continued to argue with him, pointing out the wealth and military and naval resources of Harold. They might as well have argued with the Matterhorn.'

The Norman invasion fleet was ready to sail in July, and the English defenders were ready to meet it – but then chance took a hand. Contrary winds kept William's ships in their harbours, until his men must have chafed with impatience, but the same winds brought a new player into the action, whose arrival compelled Harold to face about.

Harold's brother Tostig, a violent and unreliable man, having lost his lands as the result of a popular revolt in 1065, had turned freebooter. He prowled around the south-east coast of England for some time in early 1066, before joining

HIC RESIDET HAROLD REX: ANGLORVM: STIGANT ARCHIEPS

below
The roads built during the Roman occupation of Britain still provided the main lines of communication in the 11th century. It was along routes such as this that Harold's army travelled north to beat the invading Vikings, and then south again to meet Duke William and the Normans.

with the Norwegian King Harald Hardrada, who nourished his own ambitions for the crown of England. Their forces moved in time-honoured Viking fashion up the River Ouse to York, where they fought and won a savage battle with the locally levied troops at Gate Fulford.

Harold Godwineson was in London when it became clear that the Norwegian assault was more immediate than the Norman threat: his reaction was swift, terrible and decisive. Gathering a powerful army, he moved north by forced marches along the Roman roads to York and surprised the Viking camp

at Stamford Bridge on 25 September, five days after the struggle at Gate Fulford. The battle that followed was the greatest encounter in the whole 250-year history of the Viking invasions, and at the end of a murderous day Harald Hardrada, Tostig and most of their men lay dead on the field. Over 300 ships had brought the Norwegians to England; 24 sufficed to take the survivors back home again.

left
Stamford Bridge, on the River Derwent. Here Harold of England defeated Harald of Norway in a battle which, but for the Battle of Hastings, would have ranked as one of the decisive events of English history.

The Norman Invasion

below

Duke William's ship, with his banner at its masthead, leads the fleet across the Channel to the invasion of England. Notice the shields slung along the gunwale, and the sailor in the stern who both steers the ship with an oar and controls the sail.

Duke William had had a difficult summer. It was one thing to assemble an invasion force, eager for action and excited by prospects of plunder, but quite another to keep it together in the face of delays, accidents and frustrations. His nerve held, however, and his luck changed on 27 September, when the wind finally allowed his fleet to sail from St Valéry-sur-Somme. William himself was in a ship given to him by his wife Mathilda; it was called the Mora, and appears in the Bayeux Tapestry as a vessel of typical Viking build.

Little details recorded by the chroniclers show plainly that tension ran high in the Norman fleet, and every move that William made was significant in the eyes of his men. With the skill of an assured leader, he calmed their fears on the night crossing, and turned certain adverse incidents of the landing at Pevensey early on 28 September into morale-lifting encouragements. More practically to the modern mind, he acted swiftly but methodically to secure his bridgehead immediately he was ashore, erecting earthwork fortifications first at Pevensey and then at Hastings, which offered a better base for operations. He also set out to pillage and ravage the countryside. These were Harold's own personal lands, and William may have intended to goad his opponent into hasty action in defence of his people.

Harold heard of the Norman landing while he was celebrating his triumph at Stamford Bridge, and set

out immediately to meet the new
menace. The speed of his response
left contemporaries gasping, but has
puzzled historians, who have pointed
out that the Saxons might have done
better to recover their strength and
reorganize on interior lines of communication, rather than hastening head-
long into conflict. Harold may have
been intoxicated with his success in
the north; he may have felt obliged to
rush to the defence of his tenants; or he
may simply have been reacting with
the keyed-up explosiveness of one who
had been expecting to meet this chal-
lenge for the past nine months.

In any case, he moved south at
breakneck pace, and was in contact
with William by 13 October. His army
was a mixture of his own household
troops, battle-hardened but by now
surely very weary, and local levies
including lightly armed peasantry. By
comparison with the Normans, Harold
lacked what modern military analysts
would call firepower – supplied in the
11th century by archers – and a mobile

striking force – cavalry. In fact, the
Saxons came to Hastings to fight as
they had fought Viking marauders
since the time of Alfred the Great,
hand to hand with axes and swords
in the shield-wall.

above

*The movements of King
Harold's forces in response to
the Viking and Norman
invasions.*

9

right
Reconstruction of a helmet and face mask from the Anglo-Saxon royal burial at Sutton Hoo. Only the wealthiest could have afforded equipment as splendid as this.

below right
Norman soldiers depicted in Monreale Cathedral, Sicily. Notice the kite-shaped shields.

below
A Norman archer, with short bow and fistful of arrows.

Until modern times, at any rate, changes in the arts and techniques of warfare tended to be the product of experience, rather than theory. Peoples who lived in a state of insecurity, frequently in mortal conflict with their neighbours, developed their skills and weapons ahead of those who had the good fortune to live in relative tranquillity. England under the later Saxon kings was predominantly a land at peace, and its warriors were content to fight as their ancestors had fought against groups of Viking raiders, on foot, and hand to hand. They bore swords and spears or, in the case of the élite troops of royal or noble households, axes, and they defended themselves with round shields made of limewood, though perhaps by 1066 the kite shape with heavy metal reinforcements was becoming more usual. The well-to-do wore mailed shirts or hauberks, and conical helmets. Spears were used as throwing-javelins, as well as for thrusting, while bows further extended the fighting-range, though these were quite short, four-foot staves firing relatively light arrows. The chronicler Henry of Huntingdon records Duke William as speaking contemptuously of English bowmanship.

Norman weaponry was basically similar, if perhaps more sophisticated. Certainly the force that crossed the Channel was kitted out in fully professional style, if we are to believe the detailed depictions of the Bayeux Tapestry. The Normans seem to have been more thoroughly equipped with defensive mail, more generously protected by their kite-shaped shields. But in two essential respects they were far ahead of their English opponents.

First, they had mounted their best soldiers on horseback. The resulting mobility of manœuvre, added to the shock-value of the charge, gave the Normans an invaluable advantage against static infantry. The importance attached to this cavalry arm can be seen in the trouble that William took to transport his knights' horses in essentially ill-suited ships across the Channel.

The second development in the art of warfare, which the Normans had made peculiarly their own, was strategic. They campaigned for territory, not just for battles of encounter, and operated from fortified bases capable of withstanding sustained attack. Whereas Saxon thegns lived in handsomely decorated halls, Norman knights dwelt in fortified holds – castles, from which they dominated the surrounding countryside. William's first act after landing at Pevensey was to order the construction of a castle, the trademark of Norman military supremacy. Skilfully sited, many of these fortifications survive to the present day.

left
Conical helmet of a type similar to those worn by both sides at the Battle of Hastings.

below
The horses of the Norman knights gave them invaluable mobility after Hastings.

bottom
Norman cavalry advance to the attack.

Estimates of the strength of the two sides at Hastings vary between 3,000 and 7,000 apiece, with the Normans slightly stronger. These were small armies, to be sure, even by the standards of the times – but large enough for one of the most decisive encounters in English history.

below
A scene from the Bayeux Tapestry: a messenger brings news of Harold's movements to Duke William, who sits in military state, ready for action. The detail suggests an attempt to give an impression of the real appearance of the Norman invader.

The Saxons spent the night of Friday 13 October on a promontory of a hill jutting south-eastwards from the high forest of the Weald, nine miles (14km) from Hastings itself. The front of their position was less than a third of a mile wide (536m), and before it the ground fell away to a gentle valley. It was a ground well-chosen for conducting a stubborn defence.

William kept his troops under arms during Friday night, and marched at first light towards the Saxon encampment; in fact, it appears that he achieved tactical surprise. His early attacks from about 9.00 a.m. onwards, however, were steadily beaten off by the Saxons lining their defensive stockade.

According to Robert Wace 'loud and far resounded the bray of the horns; and the shocks of the lances, the mighty strokes of maces, and the quick clashing of swords. Now the Englishmen rush on, now they fall back; now the men from over sea charge onwards, and again at other times retreat. The Normans shouted, "Dex Aie", the English people "Out". Then came the cunning manœuvres, the rude shocks and strokes of the lance and blows of the swords, among the serjeants and soldiers, both English and Norman. When the English fall, the Normans shout. Each side taunts and defies the other, yet neither knoweth what the other saith; and the Normans say the English bark, because they understand not their speech.'

right
Mounted Norman knights attack the hilltop position of the Saxons, with severe losses to both sides. Notice the lighter equipment of the Saxons – and the different fashions in hair styles. The Saxon figures at the bottom of the hill may represent the groups who left the shield-wall in order to pursue retreating Norman cavalry.

It became clear that so long as the Saxons held firm, the Normans could not overrun them. Ironically, it was a Norman reverse that opened the way in to the Saxon position: one of the cavalry attacks having been routed with particular destruction, undisciplined elements in the Saxon line, probably among the locally raised troops, broke out in pursuit – thereby exposing themselves, and weakening the shield-wall. Perhaps twice after that, the Normans deliberately feigned retreats in order to induce the men on the hilltop to come down from their position.

above

The walls and turrets of Battle Abbey, much altered and restored over the centuries, still crown the gentle slope on which the Saxons took their stand for the Battle of Hastings. The condition of the ground has changed greatly since the fatal day, but the contours remain unaltered.

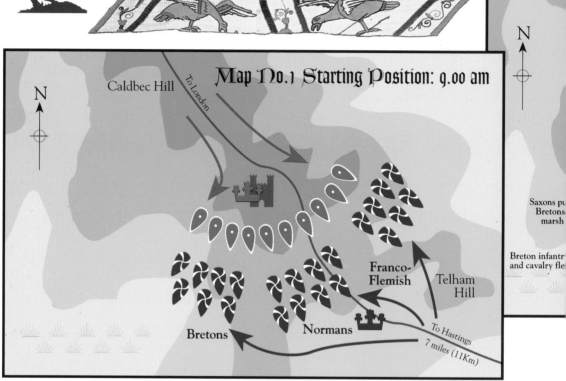

Map No.1 Starting Position: 9.00 am

Caldbec Hill

To London

N

Franco-Flemish

Telham Hill

Bretons

Normans

To Hastings 7 miles (11Km)

N

Saxons pu
Bretons
marsh

Breton infantr
and cavalry fle

MAP I shows the Saxons in position astride the road that leads from Hastings to London, while the Normans fan out to attack.

MAP II gives the position about mid-day: part of the Norman attack has recoiled in disorder and the Saxons have broken formation to pursue.

MAP III shows the final disintegration of the Saxon line around 4.00 p.m.

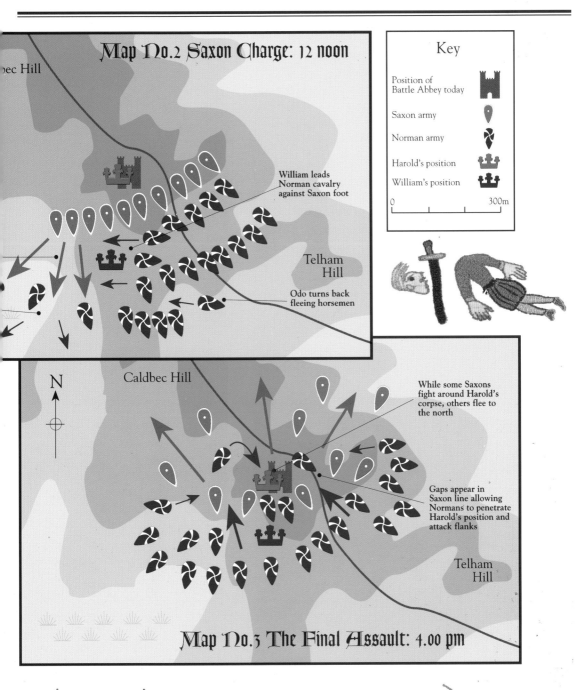

Map No.2 Saxon Charge: 12 noon

bec Hill

William leads
Norman cavalry
against Saxon foot

Telham
Hill

Odo turns back
fleeing horsemen

Key

Position of
Battle Abbey today

Saxon army

Norman army

Harold's position

William's position

0   300m

Map No.3 The Final Assault: 4.00 pm

N

Caldbec Hill

While some Saxons
fight around Harold's
corpse, others flee to
the north

Gaps appear in
Saxon line allowing
Normans to penetrate
Harold's position and
attack flanks

Telham
Hill

The Battle of Hastings

It is a mark of the importance that contemporaries, and those who came immediately after, attached to the Battle of Hastings that they wrote about it in immense detail. In fact, it has been said that we know more about Hastings than about any other medieval battle.

Robert Wace described the action thus: 'There was an Englishman who much annoyed the French, continually assaulting them with a keen-edged hatchet. He had a helmet made of wood, which he had fastened down to his coat, and laced round his neck, so that no blows could reach his head. The ravage he was making was seen by a gallant Norman knight, who rode a horse that neither fire nor water could stop in its career, when its master urged it on. The knight spurred, and his horse carried him on well till he charged the Englishman, striking him over the helmet, so that it fell down over his eyes; and as he stretched out his hand to raise it and uncover his face, the Norman cut off his right hand, so that his hatchet fell to the ground. Another Norman sprang forward and eagerly seized the prize with both his hands, but he kept it little space, and paid dearly for it, for as he stooped to pick up the hatchet, an Englishman with his longhandled axe struck him over the back, breaking all his bones, so that his entrails and lungs gushed forth.'

An episode pictured in the Bayeux Tapestry shows William raising his helmet to reassure his men that he still lived, and to rally them on. He is said to have had three horses killed under him during the day.

Eventually, the close-packed Saxon host frayed open, either because of the

above
The ruins of Battle Abbey, founded by William after his triumph at Hastings. The high altar is said to be situated where Harold fell. William and his successors lavished generous benefactions on the monastery.

distractions of the feigned retreats, or under the hail of archery, or simply by attrition – or because of all three. The struggle raged most bitterly around Harold's standard, in the centre of the Saxon position, where Harold himself, wounded in the eye by an arrow, was eventually beaten down and killed, together with his two brothers Gurth and Leofwine. Even then, resistance continued, and a late rally by dogged Saxons caused savage havoc among a body of over-eager Norman pursuers whose horses fell in a hollow in the October dusk.

William 'ate and drank among the dead, and made his bed that night upon the field'. The next day, he ordered the Norman dead to be buried. Harold's body, which was identified with difficulty, was treated at first with contempt: William was anxious to represent his enemy as a perjured usurper. Only later was the last Saxon king allowed honourable re-interment, in a church which he himself had founded at Waltham. William, for his part, founded an abbey to celebrate his victory – Battle Abbey, the remains of which mark the field to this day.

left
This illustration from a 14th-century manuscript shows the climax of the Battle of Hastings as later generations wanted to see it – Duke William slays King Harold in hand-to-hand combat.

William allowed five days for his men to catch their breath after the battle at Hastings; he seems also to have hoped that submissions would come in from the English who, however, proved slow to react. Then he moved along the coast to Romney, where he exacted reprisals for an outbreak of resistance, and Dover, where the town was burnt. He had evidently decided that he would not be obeyed until he was feared, and so Kent, inhabited by people who were traditionally foremost among the defenders of the realm ('… they say that the men of Kent are entitled to strike first; and that whenever the king goes to battle, the first blow belongs to them…'), was subjected to a thorough wasting as the Normans moved by way of Canterbury and Maidstone towards the capital. The effects of this devastation were still apparent when the Domesday survey was carried out 20 years later.

Despite the sufferings of Kent, London Bridge was held against William. So he burnt Southwark, the suburb on the south bank of the river, and turned away to encircle London with a trail of destruction. Through Surrey, Hampshire and Berkshire the Normans passed with fire and sword, before coming to cross the upper Thames at Wallingford. Then, at last, the submissions began to come in – first from Archbishop Stigand of Canterbury. North of the Thames William drove through Buckinghamshire, while a southerly detachment secured the ancient capital of Winchester, and another to the north scoured as far as Bedford. Then he swung south through Hertfordshire, and at Little Berkhamsted, south of Hertford, the majority of the remaining Saxon leadership surrendered in December.

Now London was cowed, and William entered the city to be crowned in Westminster Abbey. The ceremony took place on Christmas Day. Ealdred, Archbishop of York, officiated, and as many leading Saxons as possible were brought in for the occasion: it was clearly William's purpose at this stage to demonstrate that he was as much the choice of Saxons as of Normans.

above
The Tower of London, built by the Normans to subdue the capital.

below
The River Thames at Wallingford, where William's army crossed in its flank march on London.

a writ drawn up in English, but addressed to a port-reeve (the equivalent of the later mayor) with an unmistakably Norman name.

In March William went back to Normandy, with a clutch of Saxon 'guests', leaving his half-brother Odo in command of the occupation. The Anglo-Saxon Chronicle lamented: 'Bishop Odo wrought castles widely through this country, and harassed the miserable people; and ever since has evil increased very much. May the end be good, when God will.'

The nerves of all concerned were stretched to breaking point, however, and the service ended in chaos when guards outside the church mistook the congregation's applause for a clamour of alarm, and promptly ran amok in the city. William's reign thus began with the smoke of his subjects' burning dwellings mingling with the incense of his subservient clergy.

The months that followed were devoted to a systematic plundering of the Normans' new acquisition, in order to reward the expeditionary force and to satisfy the expectations of those at home who had provided support. The quantity of loot staggered contemporaries, and William of Poitiers says that a thousand churches in France were beneficiaries of William's generosity, at the expense of the Saxons.

Meanwhile, those of the English who were prepared to collaborate were conciliated. The liberties of London were confirmed in traditional form by

A Realm Subdued

right
The royal hunt rides out – a 14th-century depiction of King William setting forth to his favourite pastime.

below
A king inspects the progress of builders working on his castle. Scenes such as this became the mark of the Norman occupation of England. Notice the hod and trowel – unchanged today!

For a short time after his seizure of England, William seems to have made a conscious attempt to merge his new kingdom with his old duchy on more or less equal terms, offering positions in his service to Saxons as well as Normans as if he were seeking to build an Anglo-Norman state. But, as one modern authority has remarked, 'William was basically just not wanted as king by the English', and he for his part was not prepared to trust any who did not offer him total and unconditional obedience. Within months of his coronation, therefore, the new king can be found behaving as the absolute ruler of a conquered possession. South-western England was subdued early in 1068; later in the same year the Midlands were pinned down by the construction of castles along a line running from Warwick, through Nottingham to York; East Anglia was cut off by another line passing through Lincoln, Huntingdon and Cambridge. The strength of these arrangements was severely tested in the months that followed, as first Yorkshire and Northumbria, then the West Midlands, the West Country, and finally the fenlands of the east burst into revolt. The resistance in the north and the east was significantly helped by Danish armies – King Svein Estrithsson of Denmark was making his own bid for what he doubtless thought was a tottering throne.

William's counterstrokes were savage, however, and sufficient to destroy any illusions about his vulnerability. The north, in particular, was punished by so ruthless a devastation that large tracts were virtually depopulated for generations: 'peasants were slaughtered, crops in store burnt, and tools and ploughs destroyed so that no seed would be sown for the next harvest'. This was the so-called 'harrying of the north' – an act of genocide which shocked even the hardened consciences of the time. Resistance in the fens was put down with similar ferocity: when Ely, the last stronghold, fell, its defenders were blinded, mutilated or executed, though their leader, the heroic Hereward the Wake, escaped to pass into legend.

To match these acts of repression, William embarked from 1067 onwards on a systematic transfer of land from Saxon to Norman hands. To begin with, this took the form of the creation of strong blocks of territory in sensitive areas, which were entrusted to William's particularly close supporters – his half-brother Bishop Odo in Kent, or his steward William fitzOsbern in Herefordshire. But as time went on the confiscations became more and more general, until by the end of the reign there were virtually no Saxons left among the major landholders of the kingdom.

Perhaps the most significant turning-point in the whole process, in moral terms at least, came in 1070, when William plundered the monasteries of the wealth which fearful Saxons had entrusted to them. His supremacy was to be absolute, and there could be no refuge. By the same token, England was simply a resource to be exploited, and after 1072 he spent little time there.

Domesday Book

William is recorded as having visited England only four times between 1072 and his death in 1087. On each of these occasions he was much preoccupied with matters of internal and external security, but his fourth visit, in 1085–6, was noteworthy for another sort of business, namely the preparations for the great survey, catalogue or inventory which we know as the Domesday Book.

Nothing like it, at least in scale or thoroughness, had ever been attempted before, and even now the results strike the modern reader with the same sense of awe that affected the Anglo-Saxon Chronicler. 'So very narrowly did he have it [i.e. the kingdom] investigated, that there was no single hide nor a yard of land, nor indeed (it is a shame to relate, but it seemed no shame to him to do) one ox nor one cow nor one pig was there left out, and not put down in his record.' The Chronicler exaggerates in his excitement, but the detail of the survey was quite staggeringly complete.

The decision to undertake this great work was taken at Gloucester, around Christmas 1085. Exactly what purpose it was meant to serve has been much debated, but it was obviously useful in the context of revenue-raising, and, more broadly, as a clarification of the pattern of land-tenure which had been so drastically disrupted by the Conquest and its aftermath. The results were ratified by a solemn oath taken at Old Sarum on 1 August 1086 by 'all the people occupying land who were of any account all over England, whosoever's vassals they might be. And they all submitted to him and became his vassals, and swore oaths of allegiance to him . . .'. This can be regarded as the formalisation of the act of conquest, and the legal foundation of the power of the Norman monarchy.

The Domesday manuscripts – so called because they struck contemporaries as having a completeness and

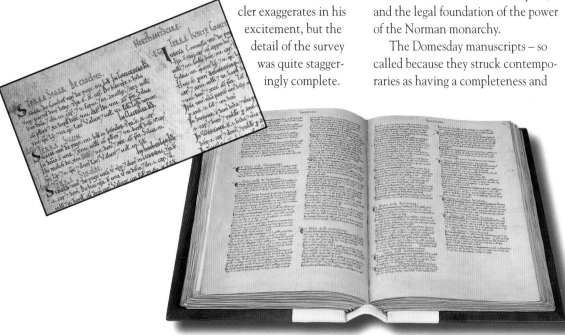

finality otherwise to be expected only at the end of the world – can be inspected today at the Public Record Office in London. There are two volumes, 'Great Domesday' covering all of England south of the Tees-Ribble line, apart from Essex, Suffolk and Norfolk, and 'Little Domesday' which deals with the three eastern counties. 'Great Domesday' is the finished product, whereas 'Little Domesday' is effectively a draft, but they are equally complete in content, if not in style.

County by county, the landholdings were listed, described and assessed for tax and general value, with comparisons drawn between 1066 and 1086. The chief towns were given distinct treatment within this scheme. The inquiries appear to have been carried out by seven teams of commissioners, who used existing (and therefore mostly Saxon) tax records as the basis for interviews with the landholders, information from which was then checked against the knowledge of local juries. It was a massively comprehensive undertaking, and powerful evidence both for the sophistication of the Saxon governmental system which made it all possible, and also for the organized ruthlessness of the Norman exploitation.

William's England: State and Society

The Norman presence in England during William's reign probably did not exceed 25,000. They were an occupying army, a colonial garrison, whose castles – whether these were royal fortresses strongly built of stone, or the hilltop stockades of the knights of the frontiers – pinned down some two million Saxons. However, the fact of occupation did not mean that English society was converted to fit a Norman model: rather, the Norman colonists assumed English roles. England was, after all, larger, richer and more settled than Normandy, and it had been in order to achieve the dignity of being king of this desirable realm that the mere Duke William had embarked on the adventure of conquest. Normans replaced Saxons in virtually all positions of power and authority: the natives manned a 'service' class, in state and Church, serving as soldiers, clerks, jurymen, moneyers and so forth. Some of the Saxons could not stomach their new roles, and, after the early rebellions had failed, there is evidence of a certain amount of emigration; most drifted into what has been called 'a resigned acceptance of defeat'. The lament for lost liberty was a persisting theme among English writers, such as the monastic chroniclers, until well into the 12th century.

One factor mitigating English bitterness, undoubtedly, was the frequency of intermarriage. Few

Norman women came over with the army – Orderic tells how in 1068 certain Norman wives begged their husbands to return, and threatened to commit adultery if they did not. In many cases those men who were free to do so married Saxon women, with the apparent encouragement of William and his lieutenants. Doubtless this contributed to the situation described by a chronicler, 'You could see many villages or town markets filled with displays of French wares and merchandise, and observe the English, who had previously seemed contemptible to the French in their native dress, completely transformed by foreign fashions.'

A matter of more precise record is the survival of English law, based on custom and consent, and the underlying English systems of land tenure and taxation. William turned all this to his own purpose, but he did not seriously attack its roots.

Of course, different parts of England felt different effects from the Conquest. Southern ports experienced growth, prosperity, an enhanced importance; for wide areas of the north, on the other hand, the coming of the Normans meant unmitigated catastrophe. Areas that looked towards France, and people who were prepared to throw in their lot with the French, benefited from William's rule at the expense of the Norse-descended parts of the population, and those regions that looked across the North Sea to Scandinavia. Thus William linked his new kingdom, not so much to Normandy – the duchy remained a separate affair, eventually passing into separate hands – but to the emergent power of France. Not till the 16th century was England to emerge from this shadow.

above
Dover Castle guards the gate of England. Fortifications may have been constructed on the site even before 1066 by Harold, and the Normans were quick to strengthen the position. The great 12th-century keep stands at the heart of concentric rings of later medieval walls and towers.

left
The effigy of William Marshal (c.1146–1219), 1st Earl of Pembroke, in the Temple Church, London. Among his achievements was the construction of the round shell keep of Pembroke Castle.

William's Last Years

right

The west front of the abbey church of St Etienne at Caen, Normandy. At once severe and aspiring, its architecture is a fitting expression of the personality of William the Conqueror, who founded the abbey and lies buried within.

The last 12 or so years of William's life were marked by a concentration of difficulties, and few marked successes. The man himself seems to have remained vigorous, purposeful and formidable to the end, but, after the days of conquest and expansion finished in the mid-1070s, he cut an increasingly dogged, defensive figure. External enemies did not cease to trouble him – King Philip I of France, who inflicted on William his one major defeat in battle, at Dol in 1076, King Malcolm III of Scotland, and King Cnut IV of Denmark – and always, somewhere or other in his wide dominions, there were groups of discontented noblemen who were prepared to risk the savage penalties handed out to unsuccessful rebels. But the most damaging source of trouble for William in his later years, as for so many great men, was his own family.

Like any other ruler of his time, William treated his close relations rather as the chairman of a great modern corporation tends to treat his board of directors; they were an interdependent group, all interested in the same property and operations, but prone to ambition and potentially violently quarrelsome. At the head of affairs, William was domineering and often terrifying, but by no means absolute in his control.

Queen Mathilda was the granddaughter of a king of France, and a formidable force in her own right. William trusted her to act for him when they were apart, and clearly respected her judgement, even when, as tended to happen in later years, she attempted to support their unruly sons. Her sudden death in 1083 greatly

Important Dates in the Life of William the Conqueror

c.1027	Born at Falaise, Normandy.
6 January 1066	Harold crowned King of England.
27 September 1066	Norman fleet sets sail.
14 October 1066	Battle of Hastings fought.
25 December 1066	Crowned King of England.
1070	The 'devastation of the north'.
1076	Defeated at Dol by Philip I of France.
1079	Wounded in battle by his son, Robert.
1083	Queen Mathilda dies.
1086	Domesday Book completed.
9 September 1087	Dies at Mantes.

weakened the family group, and affected William himself severely. He was said to have been faithful to her throughout their marriage – a rare phenomenon in those days.

William's half-brother Odo, Bishop of Bayeux, played a central role in the planning and execution of the invasion itself, and afterwards held great power as Earl of Kent, often acting as Regent in William's absence. He was an extravagant, ostentatious, insatiably ambitious character, whose scheming eventually over-reached itself in 1082 when he made a bid to become Pope, a move which William felt betrayed Norman interests. Odo spent the rest of the reign in prison.

The king's eldest son, Robert, caused severe trouble. He was dissolute, lavish and extrovert, and William withheld his trust from him – worse, he took to criticizing and deriding him in public. Not surprisingly, the young man became a focus of discontent, and stepped from insubordination into rebellion in 1078. Early in 1079 father was to be found besieging son at Gerberoi on the Norman frontier, and the two met personally in battle; William was wounded in the hand before both of them withdrew. The breach was not healed until Easter 1080, by which time the Anglo-Norman aristocracy was split from top to bottom, an ill omen when the succession came to be considered. In due course, though reluctantly, William left Normandy to Robert. His second surviving son, William, was to inherit England.

William died as violently as he had lived. In July 1087 he invaded the

French Vexin, and destroyed the town of Mantes, which had been serving as a base for raiders who had been striking into Normandy. During the aftermath of the assault, he suffered an internal injury to his stomach – he had grown very corpulent with the passing of the years – when his horse stumbled among the burning ruins. He lingered in great pain until 9 September. Upon his death, his attendants deserted the body and looted the death chamber. He was laid to rest in the abbey church of St Etienne which he had founded in Caen.

above
William's horse is startled among the burning ruins of Mantes. An imaginative reconstruction of the episode which led to the Conqueror's death.

below
The tomb of William the Conqueror in the choir of the abbey church of St Etienne, Caen.

The Verdict of History

below

The severely emphatic geometrical ornament of Durham Cathedral expresses the formidable character of the conquering Normans. The nave was begun in 1093; its stone vaulting was the first of its kind in England.

William's death was followed by a period of chaos which itself provides a judgement on the nature of his achievement. Orderic tells us that the citizens of Rouen, for instance, were totally disorientated by the news, reeling around as if drunk and then turning in panic to safeguard their possessions. The Conqueror had ruled with an iron mastery which, when it was removed, left people bewildered, insecure, irresponsible. Interestingly, the effect of his death was more marked in his own Normandy, which he had made for himself, than in England, which he had taken as it stood.

In a famous obituary, the Anglo-Saxon Chronicle praises William for his strength, and the peace which he brought in his time. 'Any honest man could travel over his kingdom without injury with his bosom full of gold, and no one dared strike another, however much wrong he had done him. And if any man had intercourse with a woman